MAPS & MAPMAKERS

MAPS & MAPMAKERS

Mapping the Seas and Airways

Martyn Bramwell

Illustrated by George Fryer

Lerner Publications Company • Minneapolis

This edition published in 1998

Lerner Publications Company
241 First Avenue North
Minneapolis MN 55401

Printed in Italy
Bound in the United States of America

Library of Congress Cataloging-in-Publication Data

Bramwell, Martyn.
      Mapping the seas and airways / by Martyn Bramwell.
            p.   cm. – (Maps & mapmakers)
      Includes index.
      Summary: Describes the history of sea and air navigation,
including the various instruments used in navigating, and current
techniques of making sea and air charts.
      ISBN 0-8225-2921-1 (lib. bdg. : alk. paper)
      1. Navigation–Juvenile literature.   Navigation (Aeronautics)–
Juvenile literature. 3. Nautical charts–Juvenile literature.
4. Aeronautical charts–Juvenile literature. [1. Navigation.
2. Navigation (Aeronautics). 3. Cartography. 4. Maps.] I. Title.
II. Series: Bramwell, Martyn. Maps & mapmakers.
VK559.3.B57   1998
629.04-5-dc21   97-12190

Acknowledgments
Thanks to Northwest Airlines for the use of the photograph on page 6; Raytheon
Marine Europe, U.K. for use of the photographs on pages 7 and 18; Cetrek Ltd.
for the top picture on page 18, the Ocean Drilling Program, U.K, for providing the
photograph used on page 22; Sonar Research and Development Ltd. for supplying
the photograph on page 27; the Natural Environment Research Council, U.K. for
the inset photograph on page 33; Lufthansa German Airlines for providing the
picture top left on page 36, the Aviation Picture Library for the inset photograph
on pages 38-39, Adrian Meredith Photography for the main picture on pages 38-
39, and the photograph on page 43. Thanks also to Mr Sam Hall, Manager,
AERAD, Heathrow Airport, London, for providing air navigation charts and
airport plans.

Contents

Introduction 7

Navigation
Landmarks and Sea Signs 8
The First Navigators 10
Dead Reckoning 12
Piloting 14
Celestial Navigation 16
Radar and Satellite Navigation 18
Navigating Underwater 20

Charting the Seas
Exploring the Oceans 22
Lead Lines and Echo Sounders 24
Hunting and Navigating with Sound 26
Mapping the Ocean Currents 28
Seabed Samplers 30
Ocean Rivers and Frozen Seas 32
Keeping an Eye on the Weather 34

Charting the Airways
Global Air Routes 36
Have a Good Flight 38
Air Navigation Charts 40
Air Traffic Control 42
Airport Plans 44

Glossary 46
Index 48

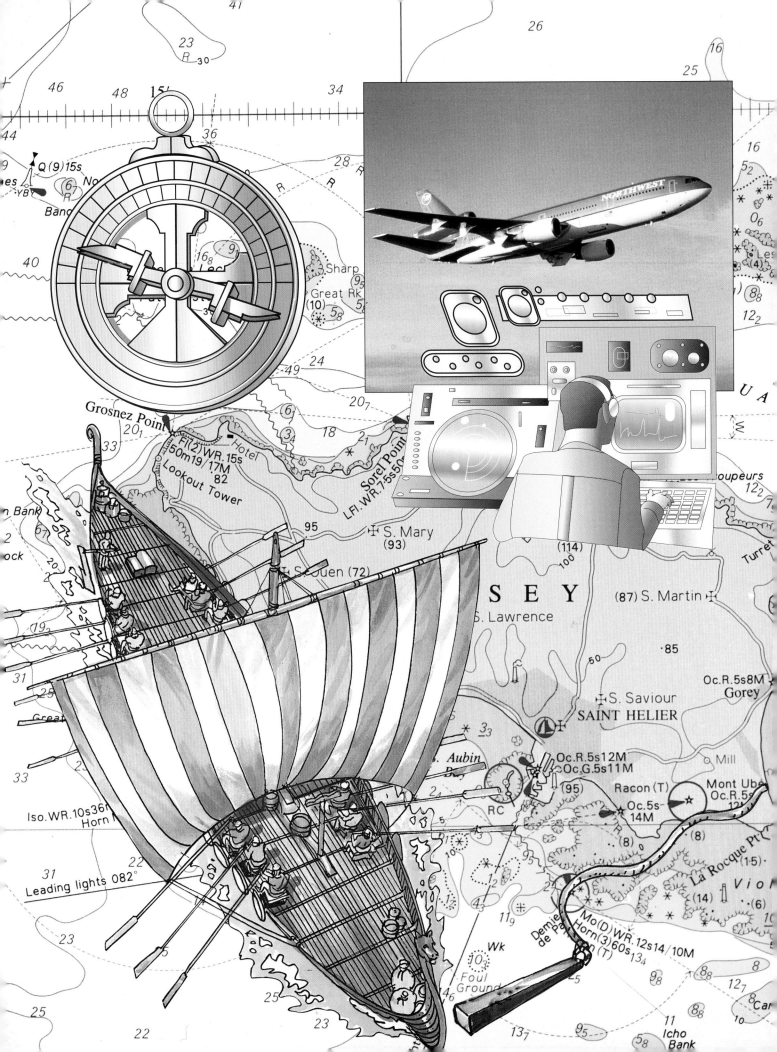

Introduction

Navigation is the science of finding out exactly where you are on the earth's surface–and then being able to find your way from there to anywhere else you may wish to go. For hundreds of years, sailors were the main users of the science of navigation, and even its name shows its seafaring origins. The word *navigate* comes from two Latin words–*navis*, which means "ship," and *agere*, which means "to drive or direct." We use the word to mean finding our way around by any method of transport–in the air, on land, on or beneath the sea, or even far out in space.

The first thing any navigator needs is a map. When used for navigating at sea or in the air, this map is more often called a chart. Other essential pieces of equipment include a compass to show directions and various instruments for drawing lines and angles, or **bearings**, on the chart. To find exactly where the ship is, the navigator can use a **sextant** and a set of tables to take measurements of the position of the sun or the stars. But most modern ships and aircraft contain radar and satellite navigation systems that automatically keep track of the vessel's position, often to within a few hundred feet.

Pilots use **air navigation charts** for finding the way from one place to another. Navigators put **sea charts** to the same purpose, but there are also dozens of other kinds of maps of the oceans and the deep seafloors. Some charts help plan where to lay undersea telephone cables and oil pipelines. Others are used in the search for minerals, oil, and gas.

Many charts guide scientific research. In fact the first detailed geology maps of the floor of the Atlantic Ocean revealed the amazing story of how the continents have been moving for millions of years–and are still on the move.

Landmarks and Sea Signs

When people first started using boats for trading and exploring, they stayed within sight of land. These seafarers had no navigational instruments–not even compasses–and had heard terrifying tales of what lay over the horizon. Some sailors believed there were monsters or banks of fog that went on forever. Others thought that near the equator the sun was so close to the earth, the sea boiled, and that people venturing too far south would burn to a cinder. Even so, from about 3000 B.C. onward, Egyptian, Greek, and Phoenician sailors were trading all along the coast of the Mediterranean Sea. By 1500 B.C., Egyptian traders were traveling down the Red Sea into the Indian Ocean and farther south along the eastern coast of Africa. Ancient wall paintings show the traders returning with gold, ivory, frankincense, and myrrh.

These early navigators found their way by memorizing coastal features such as headlands, cliffs, hills, and river mouths. After they had become familiar with a stretch of coast, they could push on and explore a bit farther. Later the navigators made sketches and lists of these features, with notes of how far apart they were. The seafarers noted which way the local winds and currents carried the ships. Soon sailors learned to use the sun and the

An Egyptian trading ship of about 1500 B.C. heads for the safety of the East African coast as a storm develops. The circling birds and floating branch show that land is not far away (in fact the lookout has just spotted it). From his viewpoint 25 feet above the deck, the lookout can see about 6 miles, a distance that is almost twice as far as the sailors on deck

stars to guide them. As the navigators became more confident, they would sail out of sight of land for several days at a time.

But the sailors still used land signs and sea signs to help them. A long pole or weighted rope to test the depth of the water would give an idea of how close to land the ship was. Shore-nesting birds flying overhead provided another clue that land was only a few miles away. Floating branches or muddy water let sailors know they were near a river mouth. Even well away from the coast, a big river could dilute the seawater enough for the difference to be tasted! It may seem odd in these days of satellite navigation, but some of these ancient skills are still used in modern times.

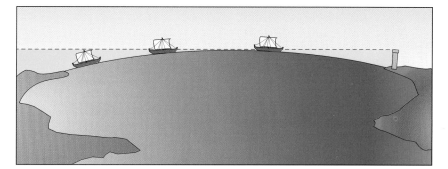

Disappearing Act

Many of the ancient Greeks believed the earth was round. Their reasoning was simple. A sphere was the only shape that could explain why ships disappeared over the horizon as they sailed away and then rose into view again as they returned.

Want to Know the Math?

ACTIVITY

If you take the height of your eye above sea level, measured in feet, multiply it by one and a half, and then take the square root of the answer, you will have the approximate distance in miles from you to the horizon.

How Far Away Is the Horizon?

The answer depends on how high up you are. For a tall person standing on tiptoe on a raft at sea, the horizon is about three miles away. For a lookout 150 feet up the mast of a clipper ship, the horizon would be 15 miles away.

The Final Proof

Scientific observation and calculations revealed 2,500 years ago that the earth is a sphere. We can see the curve from an airplane, but the first people to see the entire earth were the U.S. astronauts William Anders, Frank Borman, and James Lovell on Apollo 8 in 1968.

The First Navigators

Seafarers made some of the most amazing voyages long before scientific navigational aids were invented. People from southern Asia traveled across the sea to Australia more than 30,000 years ago, and by about A.D. 500 settlers had colonized most of the Pacific islands. These early voyagers probably made their long sea journeys in large sailing canoes. Polynesian navigators of long ago made "stick charts" of cane and seashells and used the stars to guide their voyages.

Just over a thousand years ago, the Vikings started their great journeys from their home in northern Europe westward across the Atlantic. They had only the position of the sun to estimate their **latitude**–how far north or south of the equator the ship was–yet their expeditions reached Greenland in A.D. 982 and then the coast of Labrador. Finally, in about A.D. 1000, Leif Eriksson reached mainland North America.

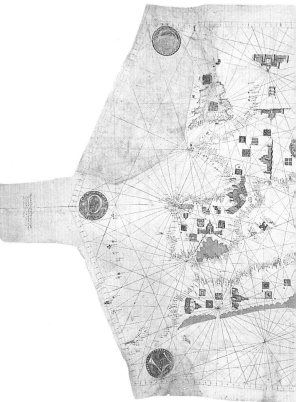

Above: A set of mathematical tables published in 1456 enabled cartographers to calculate latitude and longitude positions accurately for the first time. The new charts showed directions and distances much more precisely than earlier charts.

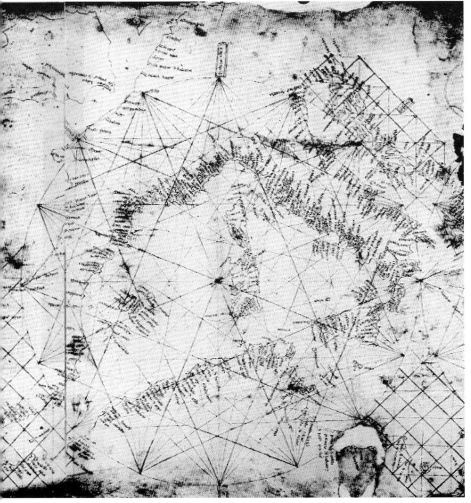

Left: The oldest known sea chart is the Carta Pisana, drawn in about 1275. It provides both compass directions and distance scales. Maps like this were used with magnetic compasses for direction finding and with sandglasses for estimating time. The charts enabled thirteenth-century navigators to travel around the Mediterranean Sea.

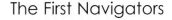

The greatest travelers of the early Middle Ages were the Arabs and the Chinese. As early as the tenth century, Arab navigators were using compasses and had astrolabes and other instruments for measuring the position of the sun and the stars. Arab traders sailed to India and China, making detailed charts of the coast of India. Chinese traders, who were the first to employ magnetic compasses, visited East Africa beginning in the eighth century–more than 600 years before the first Europeans arrived!

European navigators started late but, led by the Portuguese, they soon became the world leaders. The first real sea charts appeared in the thirteenth century. They showed coastlines, scales, and compass directions radiating out like the spokes of a wheel from various points on the chart. These charts enabled navigators to plot their course and distance accurately. Over the next few hundred years, ocean explorers charted the wind systems and main currents of the great oceans. Methods of navigating by the sun and the stars also became more precise. Even so, in the fifteenth century, navigators could calculate only their latitude because there was still no way of calculating **longitude** accurately. (To calculate longitude a navigator needs to know the precise time, but fifteenth-century clocks did not work accurately on a pitching ship. The problem was solved when the **marine chronometer** was developed in the 1730s.) Despite these difficulties, Bartolomeu Dias sailed around the Cape of Good Hope in 1488, Christopher Columbus landed on islands in the Caribbean Sea in 1492, and in 1498 Vasco da Gama sailed to India and back.

In 1492 Christopher Columbus set sail from Spain with three small ships–the *Santa Maria*, with a crew of 40, the *Pinta*, with 26 on board, and the *Nina*, with just 24. He believed that Japan lay 3,000 miles to the west, but instead of finding Japan he landed in a world that the Europeans didn't even know existed. He stopped first on San Salvador in the Bahamas and then went on to Cuba and Hispaniola before making the long voyage back to Europe.

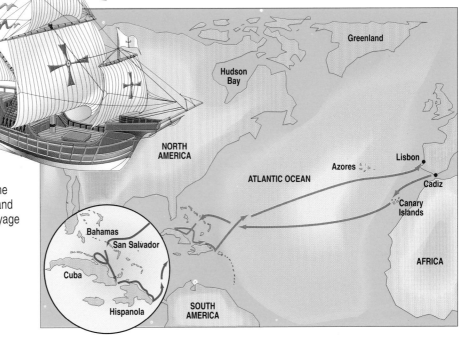

Dead Reckoning

Dead reckoning is the oldest method of navigating far from land. The navigator calculates how far the ship has traveled from its starting point and then plots that distance on a chart in the compass direction in which the ship has been traveling. This method sounds simple, but it is not very accurate. **Crosswinds** and **currents** can push the ship sideways through the water so that it ends up quite a long way from the calculated position.

In the early days of sea trading, dead reckoning was useful on big lakes and inland seas like the Mediterranean because land was never very far away. As soon as the coast was sighted, the navigator could look for a familiar landmark and quickly work out the ship's exact location. But when mariners set out to discover new lands in the fifteenth century, they needed better methods.

To calculate how far a sailing ship had traveled in an hour, the navigator had to know how fast the ship was moving. This speed could be measured using a device called a chip log. Distance is calculated by multiplying the ship's speed by the length of time

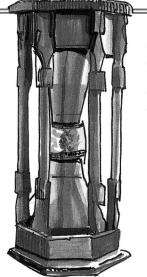

The sandglass or hourglass had two chambers joined by a narrow neck. Sand in the top chamber trickled through into the lower chamber, taking one hour to empty. A sailor would turn the glass over as soon as the last grain fell to time the next hour.

The chip log consisted of a wooden board attached to a log line, or rope, that was marked off by knots at regular intervals. The board anchored the line in the water, and the ship's movement pulled the line through the sailor's fingers. The sailor counted how many knots went through in 28 seconds. That count gave the ship's speed in **nautical miles** per hour. Even in modern times, a ship's speed is given in **knots**, with one knot equal to one nautical mile per hour.

the ship has been traveling, so the navigator also needed some way of keeping track of time. For hundreds of years, navigators relied on an hourglass, also known as a sandglass. The glass had to be turned over every half-hour or hour to keep time.

Most modern ships, including sailing boats and motor cruisers, have satellite navigation systems. But because electronic equipment can break down, sailors still learn how to navigate by dead reckoning and how to find their position using the sun and the stars. Instead of chip logs, modern ships have more accurate devices. Small boats usually have a knot-meter, a small propeller on the hull that spins in the water and measures speed. Larger ships have devices that operate on **sonar** (sound) beams bounced off the seabed or **pitot logs** that work by measuring the pressure of the water as the ship moves.

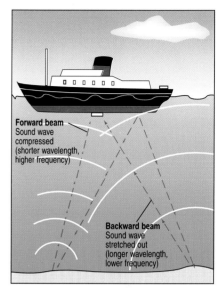

Sonar logs bounce two sound waves off the seabed, one angled downward in the direction the ship is moving and the other angled down and backward. The ship's speed alters the wavelength of the two beams. From the difference, the computer can calculate the ship's speed.

How Many Knots?

The log line was knotted at intervals of 47 feet 3 inches. That distance is the same proportion of a nautical mile (6,076 feet) as 28 seconds is of one hour (3,600 seconds). If the sailor felt five knots bump through his fingers during 28 seconds, the ship was traveling at five nautical miles an hour or five knots. The term knot is still used for the speed of a ship and for aircraft speeds, too.

Plotting a Safe Course Home

Several small islands and dangerous reefs block the direct route from Turtle Island to the mainland, and to make things worse it's getting foggy. Luckily the visiting sailor is an expert navigator. The sailor uses dead reckoning to plot a safe route on the chart, then sets off on a bearing of 55 degrees. (Bearings are given as the number of degrees measured clockwise from North.) After 28 miles, the sailor turns onto a bearing of 290 degrees for 35 miles; then onto a bearing of 235 degrees for 31 miles; and finally onto a bearing of 265 degrees for the last 28 miles back to port.

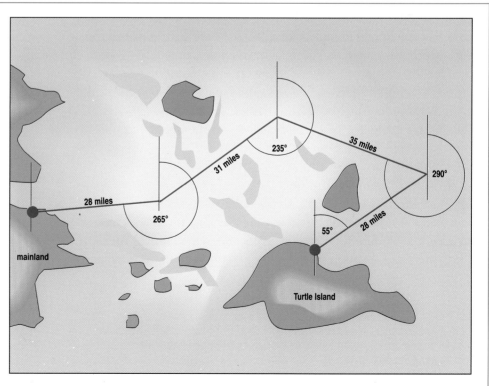

Piloting

Piloting is a method of navigation used near the coast when land is within sight. It is especially important for navigating in and out of harbors, where shipping traffic is at its busiest and where shallow waters can make navigation tricky. In piloting, the navigator plots the position of the ship in relation to one, two, or more landmarks or other reference points that can be seen from the ship. All these reference points are clearly marked on the local area sea chart. They include natural landmarks such as hills, cliffs, river mouths, points, and islands, and artificial features such as buildings, radio masts, and lighthouses. The chart also provides a detailed picture of the seabed, including the areas, called navigation channels, that are deep enough and wide enough for ships to pass through safely. In addition, the chart shows the position of any reefs, sandbanks, and old wrecks. Floating buoys, some with lights, bells, or sirens, mark these danger areas as well as the safe navigation channels.

To find the ship's position, the navigator measures the directions, or bearings, of at least two landmarks on the coast using an instrument called an azimuth circle or pelorus. The simplest kind consists of a sighting bar that can be moved in a circle over a baseplate marked off in degrees. The navigator aims the sighting bar at a landmark and reads off the angle on the baseplate. This reading gives the angle between the landmark and the center line of the ship. Depending on which way the ship is pointing, the navigator then adjusts this reading to obtain a true compass bearing measured from North. More advanced instruments have a telescopic aiming device and a built-in compass. Lenses inside the instrument display the compass bearing in the viewfinder so the navigator can read off the bearing without looking away from the telescope.

Finally the navigator plots the bearings on the chart. A **position line** is drawn out to sea from each of the landmarks in turn, and the point where the lines cross gives the position of the ship. Piloting can be done at night as well as during the day, either by using the pelorus to measure the bearings of lighthouses and lighted navigation buoys or by using the image of the coast on the ship's radar screen. A transparent scale like a protractor allows the navigator to measure the bearing from the ship, at the center of the screen, to headlands and other features that show up on the screen.

Right: This sea chart shows the coastal waters off Saint Malo in Brittany, northern France. Water depths are marked in meters and by depth of color. The radio mast just outside Saint Malo and the two big water towers on the headland are perfect reference marks for navigators using the piloting method.

Inset: A navigator prepares to take a bearing with an azimuth circle.

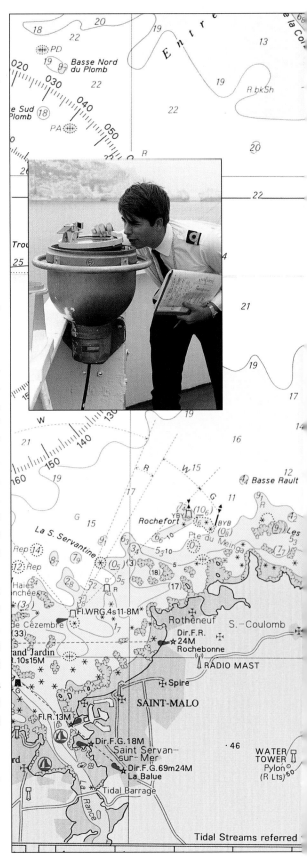

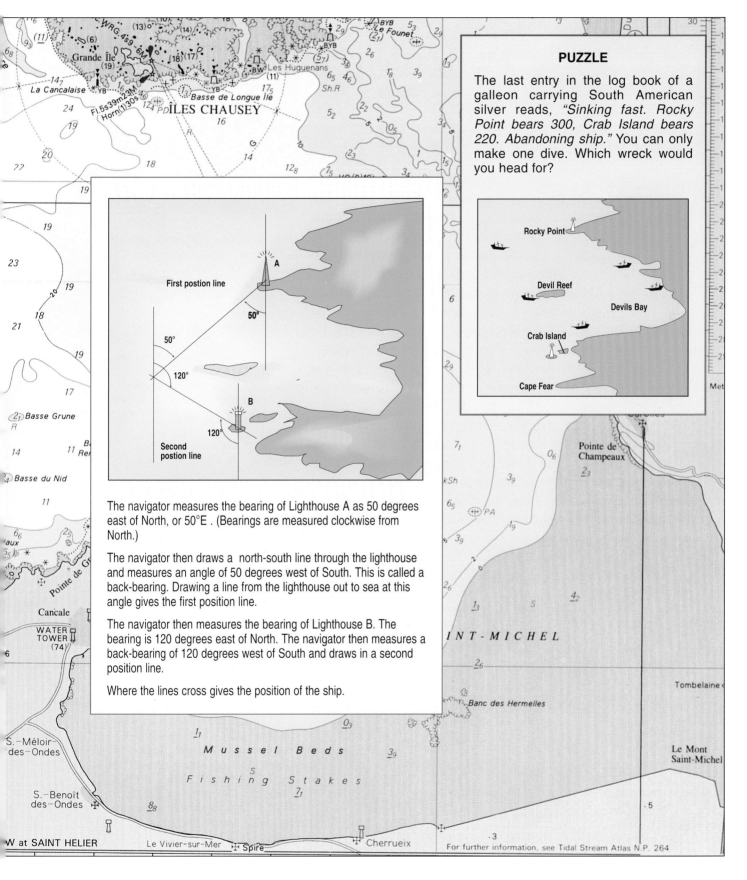

First postion line

50°

50°

120°

Second postion line

120°

A

B

Rocky Point

Devil Reef

Devils Bay

Crab Island

Cape Fear

The navigator measures the bearing of Lighthouse A as 50 degrees east of North, or 50°E . (Bearings are measured clockwise from North.)

The navigator then draws a north-south line through the lighthouse and measures an angle of 50 degrees west of South. This is called a back-bearing. Drawing a line from the lighthouse out to sea at this angle gives the first position line.

The navigator then measures the bearing of Lighthouse B. The bearing is 120 degrees east of North. The navigator then measures a back-bearing of 120 degrees west of South and draws in a second position line.

Where the lines cross gives the position of the ship.

Celestial Navigation

For hundreds of years, sailors have navigated across the oceans using the sun, the moon, and other planets and stars to guide them. The stars and planets are called celestial bodies, so these methods are known as celestial navigation.

In the first days of sailing, the main guiding stars were the sun and the North Star, and navigators used simple instruments to measure the angle between the star and the horizon. Two of the earliest instruments were the quadrant and the astrolabe. Both were heavy brass instruments that had to be held up at eye level while the navigator aimed a sighting bar at the star. They were fine in calm weather but were difficult to use in rough seas! The cross-staff was lighter and easier to use on a pitching ship. It was a wooden staff about three feet long, with a sliding crosspiece. The staff was aimed about halfway between the star and the horizon, and the crosspiece was slid along until the top end covered the star and the bottom touched the horizon. The angle, which was read off a scale marked on the staff, was used to calculate the ship's latitude.

Above: The navigator holds the sextant in both hands and lines it up on the horizon, looking through the clear part of the half-mirrored disk in front of the eyepiece. The navigator then moves the pivoted arm back and forth until the image of the star the navigator wants to measure appears in the half-mirror side of the disk. When the two images are side by side, the star's altitude can be read off the curved scale. The main scale gives the angle in degrees. The micrometer is a fine scale that can be read in minutes, that is in sixtieths of a degree.

Above left: To measure the altitude of a star with a quadrant, the navigator sighted along the top edge. An assistant would read off the altitude angle where the plumb line crossed a scale engraved on the lower edge.

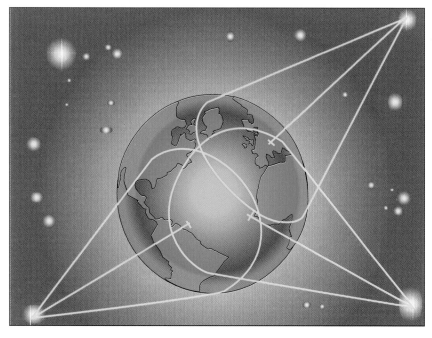

Left: Each sextant reading allows a circle of position to be drawn. Two circles give two possible positions for the ship because the circles cross in two places. Although this sounds confusing, it would not be in reality because the two points are hundreds of miles apart. The navigator would know at which of the two locations the ship was likely to be. Three circles create no problem because there is only one place where all three circles cross.

In the eighteenth century, celestial navigation improved enormously with the invention of the **reflecting quadrant** and then of the sextant. These instruments enabled navigators to measure star angles more precisely. The instruments were also used with much more accurate nautical almanacs–books of tables giving the positions of all the main stars and planets throughout the year. These days, when a navigator wants to check a position (called obtaining a fix), he or she takes a **sun sight** or **star sight** and uses this and the almanac to plot a circle of position on the chart. The center of the circle–the star's geographic position–is the spot on the earth where the star is directly overhead. The circle itself joins all the places from which a star will have the same altitude, or angle, above the horizon. The ship can be anywhere on the star's circle of position, so the navigator takes sightings on one or two more celestial bodies. When their circles of position are drawn on the chart as well, the point where the circles cross gives the ship's position.

The cross-staff was light and easy to use, but like the quadrant it could only take star and moon sights. The sun is far too bright to be looked at directly.

The sextant uses mirrors to reflect an image of the sun. It also has glare filters. This makes it safe.

Never try to look directly at the sun with a home-made instrument.

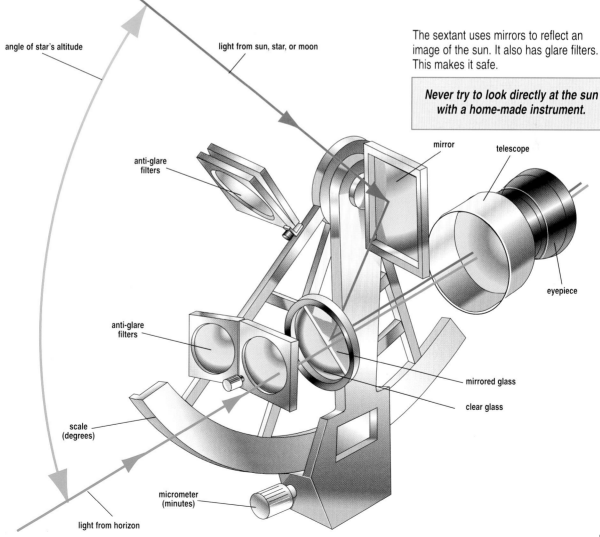

angle of star's altitude

light from sun, star, or moon

mirror

telescope

anti-glare filters

eyepiece

anti-glare filters

mirrored glass

clear glass

scale (degrees)

micrometer (minutes)

light from horizon

Radar and Satellite Navigation

These days most navigation systems are based on devices that listen for radio signals transmitted by navigation beacons on land or by satellites orbiting high above the earth. These electronic navigation systems are amazingly accurate. Even the simplest ones can fix the position of a ship or aircraft to within one-tenth of a mile, while the most accurate military systems can tell a navigator where a ship or plane is to within a few yards! By contrast an eighteenth-century navigator using star sights would be doing well to fix a ship's position to the nearest 35 miles. Another enormous advantage of electronic navigation is that radio signals pass straight through clouds and fog. This means that planes can land even when they can't see the ground, and ships can navigate safely into harbor in dense fog using radar and radio navigation aids.

Radio direction finding (RDF), one of the first electronic systems, is still widely used by aircraft and ships, especially when they are close to the coast. A rotating antenna on the ship picks up the signal and indicates the direction from which the signal is coming. Another popular system is Loran (*LO*ng *RA*nge *N*avigation), which ships and aircraft employ as they approach the coast from far out at sea. This system requires two types of transmitters–"master stations" and "slave stations"–which continually send out signals. Special equipment on the ship picks up the signals from a master station and one of its slaves and uses the signals to plot a line of position on a chart. The equipment then plots a second line of position using signals from the master station and a second slave. Where the two position lines cross is the ship's position. A third system, called Omega, is an international joint effort. With eight powerful transmitters spaced around the world, Omega can help a ship fix its position by plotting lines of position from signals from any two stations.

The most advanced navigation system is the U.S. Navstar, which consists of 21 satellites placed in six different orbits about 12,550 miles above the earth. Using signals from any three satellites, a computer on board a ship or aircraft can calculate its position to within about 50 feet.

Above: The Chartnav can store up to six complete routes, along with details of 500 navigation markers such as lighthouses and buoys. The navigator can move around the chart using a trackball and can zoom in for a close-up of a harbor entrance or out again to see the whole route.

Below: A sailor at the chart table of a small boat has two radar screens mounted above the chart table.

Right: Most modern ships and boats are equipped with radar. The navigator of a large ferry checks the harbor traffic on a large screen.

Navigating Underwater

A modern submarine may have to stay underwater for weeks or even months at a time. This means the navigator must be able to fix the submarine's position and plot its course without surfacing. If absolutely necessary, the navigator could come close to the surface and take star sights through a special periscope or pick up the signals from navigation satellites by poking the submarine's radio aerials above the water. But these options could be dangerous. Enemy ships might spot the submarine. What the navigator needs is a self-contained system that doesn't require any information from the outside world. That system, called **inertial navigation**, is so accurate and so reliable that large passenger planes and spacecraft also use it.

The heart of the inertial navigator is a gyroscope, which is a heavy metal wheel that spins like a top at several thousand revolutions per minute. An unusual feature of any spinning object is that as long as it keeps on spinning, its axis will try to remain pointing in the same direction. Inside a gyroscope, a framework of rings called gimbals supports the wheel. The rings move freely in any direction, so the whole framework can tilt, turn, and roll, but the wheel will remain in exactly the same position inside it.

Nearly all large modern ships have a gyrocompass–a gyroscope set with its axis pointing north-south. The framework is attached to the ship, so whenever the ship changes direction, sensors measure the difference between the direction of the frame and the direction of the gyroscope's axis. This information is relayed to the ship's bridge, where a dial displays the ship's compass heading.

A full inertial navigation system has three gyroscopes with their axes at 90 degrees. The gyroscopes are attached to a computer, which tracks their exact positions. Additional sensors called accelerometers detect every slight change in the vessel's speed and direction, feeding this information to the computer. After the system is set up, it automatically monitors the vessel's position no matter how many times the ship changes direction or speed.

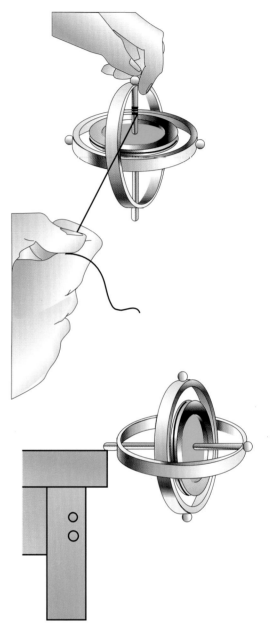

The gyroscopic top is started by winding a string around the spindle and pulling it firmly. The wheel is heavy with a thick rim, and it spins very fast. After the top has begun spinning, it will remain balanced in the most surprising positions.

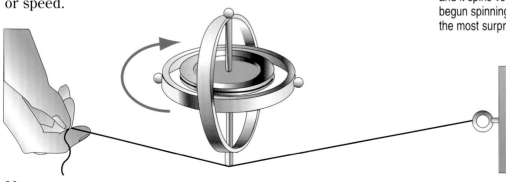

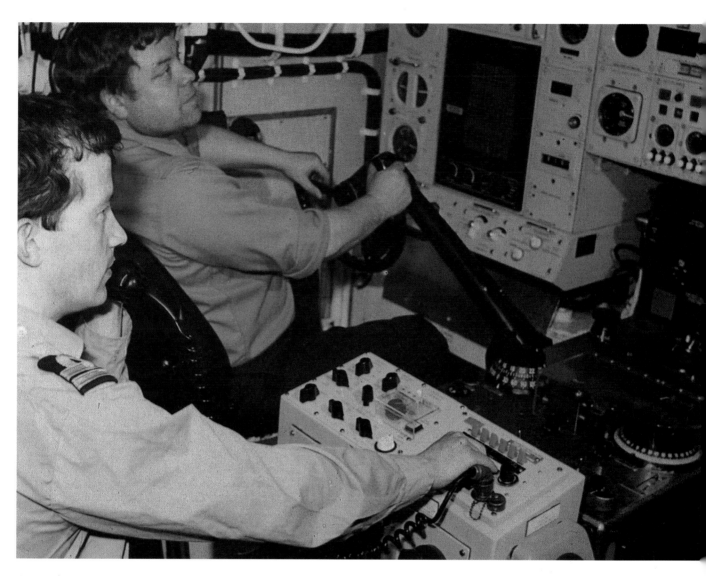

Above: Submarines spend most of their time in the dark, silent world of the deep oceans. They rely on their electronic eyes and ears to know what is going on around them and on inertial navigation equipment to know where they are.

Below: The wheel of a big ship's gyrocompass can weigh up to 50 pounds, and an electric motor keeps it spinning at several thousand revolutions per minute. The wheel spins inside a cradle of gimbals with their pivots at right-angles to each other, so that no matter which way the ship pitches or rolls, the axis of the wheel continues to point in the same direction.

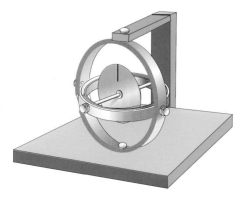

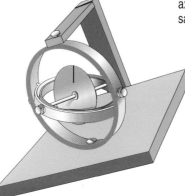

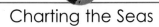

Exploring the Oceans

The *Resolution*, the world's most advanced drilling vessel, has taken thousands of rock samples from the deep seabed all over the world.

Scientists on HMS *Challenger* had few modern research tools–just their microscopes, notebooks, and a great thirst for knowledge.

Water covers almost 71 percent of the earth's surface. Yet the swirling ocean currents, the life of the oceans, and what lies on the deep seafloor remained hidden until well into the nineteenth century.

The great voyages of exploration between the fifteenth and eighteenth centuries opened up the whole world. In 1492 Christopher Columbus reached the Americas. Between 1519 and 1522, Ferdinand Magellan's expedition sailed around the world for the first time. And between 1768 and 1780, Captain James Cook charted the coasts of Australia and New Zealand and explored the islands of the Pacific Ocean. These great navigators were the pathfinders for the scientific age that followed.

In 1872 a very different kind of expedition set out from Britain. HMS *Challenger* was a former warship converted into a floating laboratory. The ship carried hundreds of bottles for collecting samples of seawater and marine animals and plants, long weighted **lead lines** for measuring the depth of the water, and assorted nets and baskets for catching specimens. *Challenger*'s three-and-a-half year mission was to explore the oceans, not simply to sail across them. This expedition started the new

science of oceanography–the study of the oceans. Since then marine geologists, biologists, chemists, and physicists have delved deeper and deeper into the oceans, using more advanced technology year by year.

In the last 30 years, these scientists have made astonishing discoveries. Studies of the seafloor have shown that the earth's crust (outer layer) consists of huge slabs which are slowly moving. These slabs are changing the shape of the oceans and pushing up mountain ranges. Explorers have found strange worms living in scalding hot water that gushes out of seabed volcanoes. Machines have drilled holes more than a mile into the seafloor. And research ships and satellites have mapped everything from ocean currents and storm tracks to fisheries and mineral resources.

Above: Scientists use oceanographic submersibles, with and without crews, to study the geology and life of the deep oceans. Underwater photography is used extensively so that features of the seabed can be recorded and kept as permanent records.

Below: This amazing image of the Pacific Ocean, taken by the Seasat satellite, shows the huge mountains and deep trenches on the ocean floor.

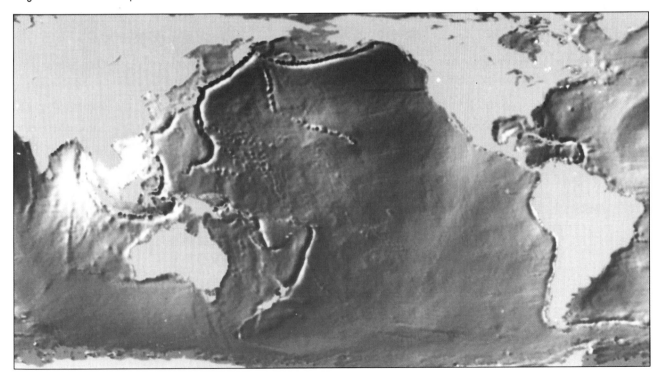

Lead Lines and Echo Sounders

One of the first people to start mapping the oceans properly was the U.S. geographer Matthew Fontaine Maury. During the 1840s, he produced charts showing the winds, currents, and water depths around the coasts of North America. These charts made navigating near the U.S. coast much safer, especially for sailing ships that carried most of the world's cargo at the time. He also produced the first map showing the shape of the entire Atlantic Ocean floor. Maury made his charts by measuring the depth of the water at many different places using a lead line–a long rope with a lead weight at the end. The traditional lead line was marked off in fathoms (one fathom is equal to six feet) by pieces of colored cord or cloth tied to the main line. Different colors marked the hundreds to help the person monitoring the lead line keep count. Later versions used steel piano wire instead of rope.

Scientists used this method of measuring water depth until the 1900s. The method was accurate enough for charting shallow estuaries and coastal waters, which are the most dangerous areas for ships as they head for port. But the method was not so accurate in the deep oceans. There the line would often be pulled out sideways by deep-water currents, giving inaccurate readings.

In the 1920s, inventors came up with a new device called an echo sounder that uses sonar–*SO*und *NA*vigation and *R*anging. This tool works by sending out a pulse of sound and then measuring how long it takes for the echo to bounce back from the seabed or any other solid object under the water. Scientists use the time it takes for the echo to return to figure out how far away the seabed or object is.

Mark Twain!

Samuel Langhorne Clemens, one of America's greatest writers, took his pen name from the cry of the linesmen on Mississippi riverboats. (In his twenties, Clemens was a licensed riverboat pilot.) The shout of "mark twain" meant the linesman was reading the second marker on the lead line, indicating a water depth of two fathoms (12 feet).

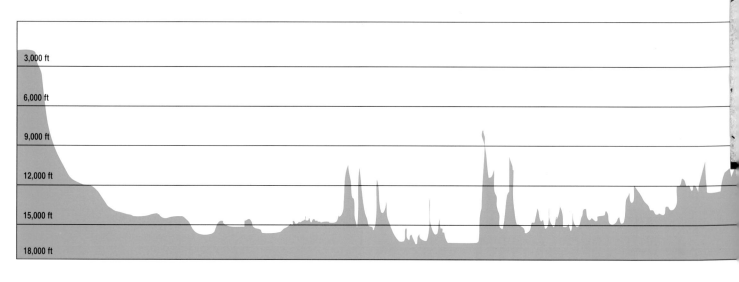

3,000 ft

6,000 ft

9,000 ft

12,000 ft

15,000 ft

18,000 ft

Sonar's original purpose was to detect enemy submarines during World War II. Later improvements made sonar accurate enough to be used for surveying the seabed. Modern sonar equipment can measure depths of 18,000 feet to the nearest 6 feet! Since the 1950s, sonar has been the main tool for making marine charts and for navigating safely in shallow waters.

Modern warships are equipped with several different kinds of sonar. Crew members use depth-recording sonars to navigate safely through shallow waters, but the ships also have sensitive attack and defense sonars for detecting enemy submarines.

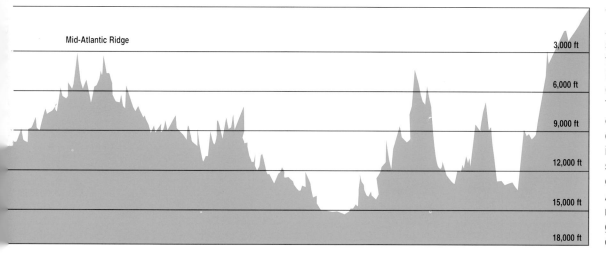

Mid-Atlantic Ridge

3,000 ft

6,000 ft

9,000 ft

12,000 ft

15,000 ft

18,000 ft

This cross section of the Atlantic Ocean shows the shape of the seafloor from Cape Hatteras, North Carolina, to Gibraltar, near Spain. The vertical scale is exaggerated, but the diagram gives a good idea of the spectacular scenery beneath the oceans. The huge Mid-Atlantic Ridge is 1,000 miles wide in places–the greatest mountain range on our planet.

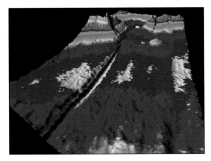

Above: This three-dimensional (3-D) sonar image shows a submarine pipeline in a trench on the seabed. The trench can be seen to pass between two ridges in the background. Bright colors indicate the depth of the seabed and assist in reproducing the 3-D image.

Below: Side-scan sonar provides a three-dimensional picture of the seabed. Sound transmitters and receivers are mounted inside a torpedo-shaped "fish," which is towed behind the ship about 130 feet underwater. Sometimes (as shown here) the transmitters are mounted in the ship's hull. The transmitters send out two fan-shaped beams of sound waves–one on each side of the ship. (Only one of them is shown here.) The ship's onboard computer analyzes the echoes to build a picture of the seabed.

Hunting and Navigating with Sound

Some parts of the deep ocean floor are featureless, flat, muddy plains, but all the world's oceans contain mountain ranges and deep trenches as well as islands poking up through the water from the seabed far below. To find their way safely through this underwater world, submarine navigators need accurate seabed charts.

The submarine's electronic eyes and ears are its sonar systems. Some systems, called passive sonar, simply listen for the engine and propeller sounds of other vessels. Passive sonar keeps totally silent to avoid giving away the submarine's own position. Active sonar, on the other hand, sends out "pings" and measures the time it takes for their echoes to return. Downward-looking sonar measures the depth of water beneath the submarine. Forward- and rearward-looking sonars allow the crew to see obstructions (and other submarines) ahead or behind them. And some submarines also have upward-looking sonar enabling them to navigate safely under polar ice caps.

Submarine navigators also need charts and cross sections showing the depth and temperature of the water. Sudden changes in water temperature can interfere with the way sonar works, and a submarine can actually hide beneath these thermal layers.

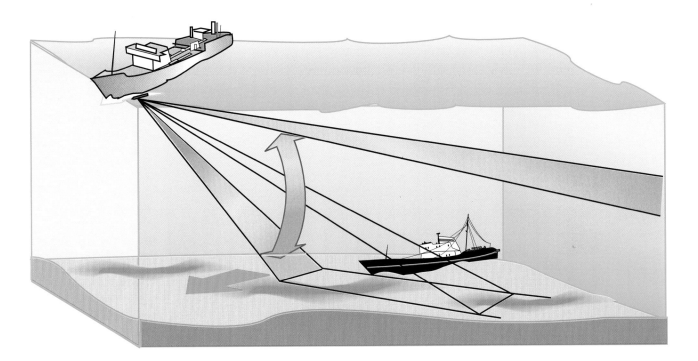

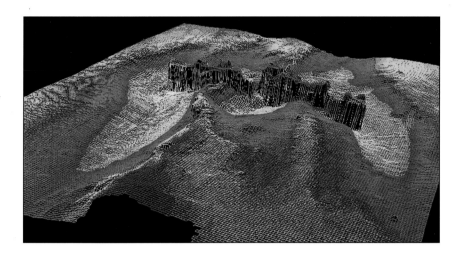

Another type of sonar, called side-scan sonar, sweeps a fan-shaped beam of sound waves outward at either side of the ship and uses computer-processing to build a three-dimensional picture of the sea bed from the returning echoes. Uses of side-scan sonar include scientific research, surveying underwater pipeline routes, and finding wrecks and lost anchors on the seabed.

Deep-sea fishing also makes use of sonar technology. Most modern trawlers and seine boats carry sonar equipment for finding fish shoals. Many boats also have small sonar units fixed to the nets themselves. This enables the captain to adjust the height of the net above the seabed and even to adjust the size of the net opening to obtain the biggest catch.

Left: Found it! Salvage experts used a hull-mounted scanning sonar system to create this three dimensional image of a wrecked ship lying broken in two pieces on the seafloor.

Fishing with Sound Waves
Fishing crews know that some fish gather over shallow sandbanks. Some fish like gravel, while others prefer deep water. The captain will use normal charts of water depth to navigate to a chosen fishing ground. Then the captain turns to sonar for the final hunt.

First, the shoal shows up as a dense patch of echoes on the echo sounder. The echoes tell the captain exactly how far above the seabed the fish are swimming. Then, using a second echo sounder mounted on the net, the captain can adjust the height and the size of the net opening and steer the net right onto the target for a big catch. (The most advanced sonar can also tell how big the shoal is—and even what kind of fish are down there!)

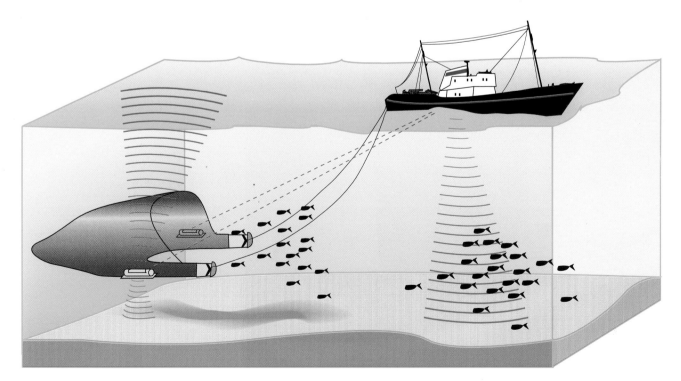

Mapping the Ocean Currents

The first sailing ships were small and crowded. They carried only a limited amount of food and fresh water, so their navigators had to make good use of the winds and currents if the ships were to reach their destination before supplies ran out. Later, when big sailing vessels like the clipper ships carried most of the world's trade, sea captains who could sail faster than their rivals could become rich quickly. Because understanding the ocean currents was a very important part of navigation, currents were one of the first ocean features to be mapped.

Close to shore, most currents are caused by the tides as they surge in and out twice a day. As the tide rises, the water sweeps into bays and estuaries and swirls around headlands, sometimes gouging deep channels where the water flows very fast. These local currents can be tricky, and that is why local pilots usually navigate big ships in and out of ports.

Once out at sea, navigators concentrate on the great ocean currents, which are driven by the winds. North and south of the equator, they form roughly circular systems called gyres, which rotate clockwise in the Northern Hemisphere and counterclockwise in the Southern Hemisphere. Relatively warm, light water flows outward from the equator, and cold, heavy, very salty water flows toward the equator from the polar regions.

Below: Even modern supertankers and freighters take advantage of ocean currents. The currents reduce the amount of expensive fuel the big ships need to burn. This high-tech Japanese tanker also uses computer-controlled sails, like aircraft wings, to get assistance from the wind.

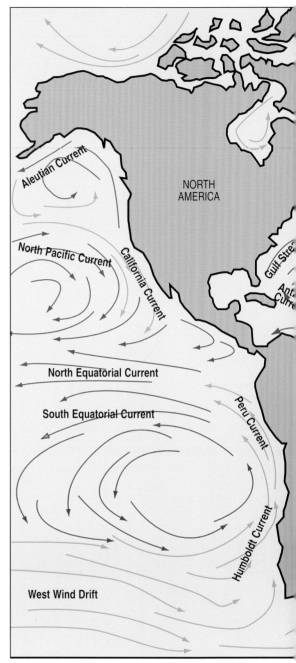

Above: A map showing global ocean currents (above) and a map depicting global wind patterns look very similar. Because winds drive the surface waters, they keep the currents circulating.

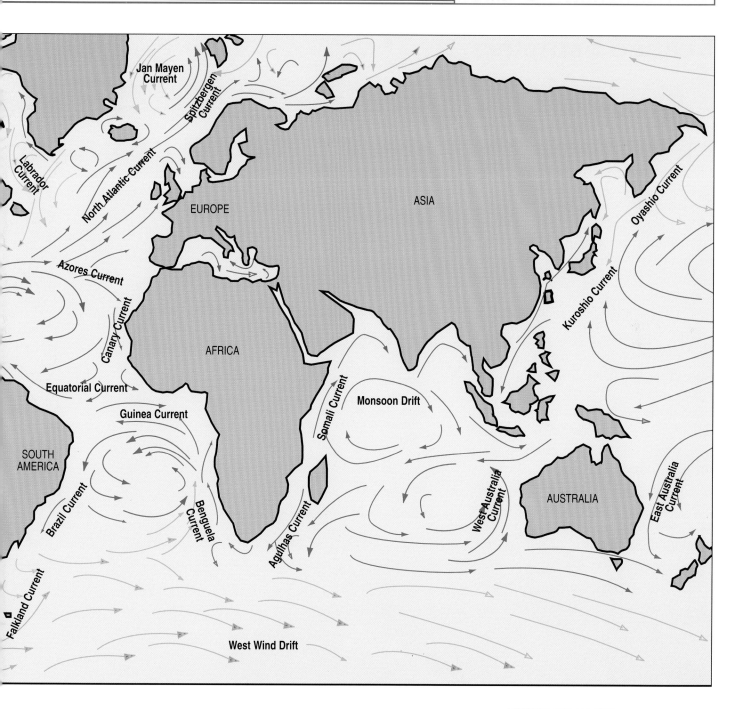

These days experts usually map currents by measuring the temperature and saltiness of the water in many different places and then use computers to predict how the warm light water and heavier cold water will move. Special buoys that float beneath the surface can measure deep ocean currents. The buoys send out sonar signals that allow the buoys' movements to be tracked from ships. Another method uses automatic current recorders that can be left on the seabed for months at a time.

Becalmed!

Early sailors had to beware of getting caught in the doldrums along the equator and the horse latitudes at about 30°N and 30°S. These regions have very weak currents and long periods with hardly any wind. As a result, sailing ships could easily become stranded for days or even weeks on end.

Seabed Samplers

Bouncing sound waves off the seabed provides a good picture of the underwater landscape, but scientists also want to know exactly *what* is down there. To obtain this information, scientists must collect samples.

Geologists want to know what kinds of sediments (sand, silt, and mud) are covering the bottom and what kinds of rocks are hidden beneath the sediment. They get their answers with a variety of bottom samplers. Ships drop these heavy devices onto the seabed where they take a bite out of the bottom sediments or drive a hollow pipe into the seabed to take out a long core sample. The sampler is then hauled back to the surface. To find out what lies even farther down, scientists can drill boreholes from special drilling ships.

Taking samples in this way helps scientists understand the geological processes taking place on the deep seafloor. Samplers can also be used to

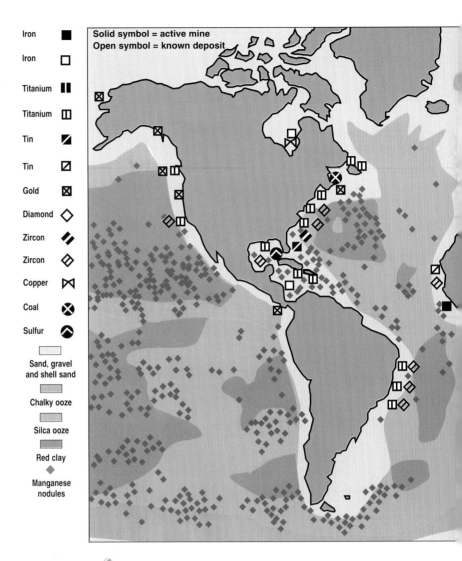

Iron ■
Iron □
Titanium ❚❚
Titanium ❑❑
Tin ◪
Tin ◪
Gold ⊠
Diamond ◇
Zircon ❖
Zircon ◈
Copper ⋈
Coal ⊗
Sulfur ◓

Sand, gravel and shell sand

Chalky ooze

Silca ooze

Red clay

Manganese nodules

Solid symbol = active mine
Open symbol = known deposit

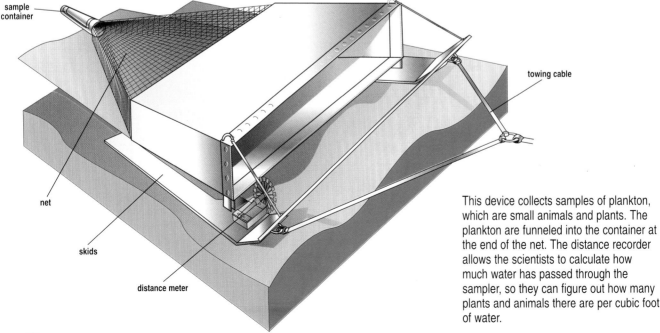

sample container

towing cable

net

skids

distance meter

This device collects samples of plankton, which are small animals and plants. The plankton are funneled into the container at the end of the net. The distance recorder allows the scientists to calculate how much water has passed through the sampler, so they can figure out how many plants and animals there are per cubic foot of water.

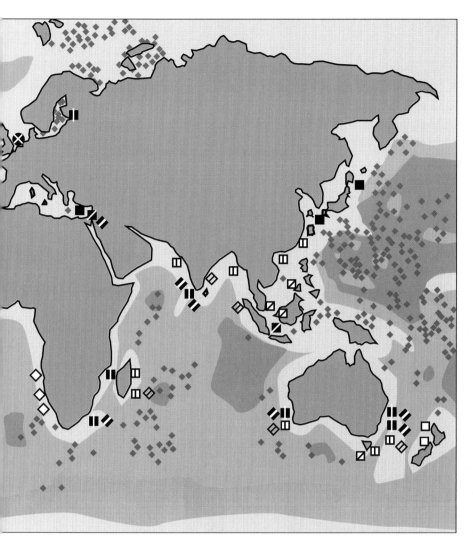

find deposits of some of the minerals needed by industry. In many parts of the world, rivers have washed valuable minerals into offshore sandbanks from which miners have begun to extract tin, titanium, iron, and sulfur. More deposits are being discovered all the time. Marine geologists have also found that some parts of the deep ocean floor are covered with nodules (rounded lumps) rich in manganese, copper, and nickel.

Less than 200 years ago, people thought that nothing could live more than a few hundred feet underwater. But by lowering sampling nets and other devices deep into the oceans, marine biologists have discovered that there are worms, crabs, sponges, starfish, and a whole range of strange-looking fish in the deepest parts of the oceans–even in the scalding water near undersea volcanoes.

Seabed Resources

The symbols on the map show the main areas where geologists have found useful minerals in sandbanks close to land. Huge floating dredgers mine the sandbanks. Near the coast, the seabed is covered in sand and silt that has been washed off the land. The deep ocean sediments are made of the shells and skeletons of microscopic sea creatures. These fine muds (called oozes) build up very slowly–often adding less than half an inch in 1,000 years–yet they are hundreds of feet thick in some places.

Right: When the core sampler hits the seabed, the tube is pushed into the sediment. As the cables are pulled tight, the spade swings down and closes off the tube so the sample does not fall out as the core sampler is hauled back to the surface.

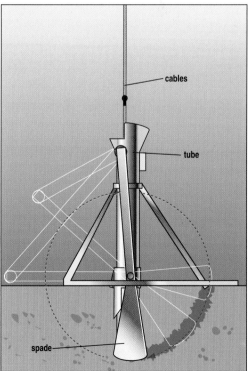

cables

tube

spade

Ocean Rivers and Frozen Seas

Satellite technology has provided scientists with many new ways of studying the oceans. Some satellite cameras take pictures with visible light (a form of light that humans can see). Infrared cameras can see things humans can't see, such as differences in ocean water temperature, and these photographs allow areas of warm and cold water to be mapped. Other instruments measure the colors (wavelengths) of light reflected from seaweed beds along the coasts, and from masses of floating plankton.

Plankton are the main food for fish and other sea creatures, so maps showing the distribution of plankton help fishing crews plan where to fish. The maps also aid biologists and conservationists in understanding changes in fish populations so the scientists can provide a warning if too many fish are being caught.

The National Weather Service uses infrared satellite photographs to map the changes in the Gulf Stream–the swift, warm current that flows like a huge river from the Caribbean Sea up the coast of North America and then across the North Atlantic. The size, shape, and position of the current are constantly changing and so the maps are extremely useful to marine biologists, sailboat navigators, U.S. Coast Guard search-and-rescue teams, and marine-pollution investigators.

Satellite maps of cold and warm ocean currents have also helped to explain El Niño, the name given to the strange changes that take place in the waters off Ecuador and Peru every few years. The waters are usually cold and very rich in fish, but every two to seven years the current changes suddenly, and warm water sweeps down the coast from the equator. El Niño kills much of the plankton, with disastrous effects on the fish and the local fishing industry. Scientists have learned that this change in the ocean current pattern is felt as far away as Australia.

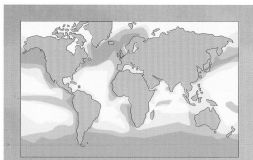

Plankton Grow Best in Cold Water.
On this map, the stronger the color, the more plankton is in the water. The richest areas are along coasts where there are cold currents. Zones of cold water in the far northern and southern oceans are also rich in plankton. See if you can find out where most of the world's fish supplies are caught. Is there a link between these fishing spots and the plankton-rich cold zones?

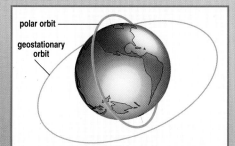

Geostationary satellites are used mainly for communications. These satellites orbit 22,300 miles above the equator and make one circuit in 24 hours–the same time it takes the earth to revolve once. The result is that the satellites always remain directly over the same spot on the earth. This is important because if the satellite disappeared around the "back" of the earth, it could not be used to relay communications signals. Satellites in polar orbits pass over the North and South Poles on each circuit, and over a period of about 18 days they see all of the earth's surface. Polar-orbiting satellites are ideal for making maps and studying large-scale features such as weather systems, currents, and polar sea-ice.

Right: Every summer in the Southern Hemisphere, research ships carry teams of scientists to Antarctica. Pack ice and wave-worn fragments of icebergs are a constant danger. To navigate safely through the Southern Ocean, the ships' captains use satellite pictures of the floating pack ice.

Right: This infrared picture covers an area from New York (at the top) to North Carolina (at the bottom). Computer-generated colors indicate the temperature of the water and pick out the ocean currents. The picture shows the point where the cold Labrador Current (blue and purple), flowing down from the Davis Strait, meets the warm Gulf Stream (red and orange), flowing up the U.S. coast from the Caribbean. The Labrador Current blocks the Gulf Stream and forces it to flow northeastward across the Atlantic.

Keeping an Eye on the Weather

Modern technology has made weather forecasting faster and more accurate than anyone could have imagined. Computers can carry out millions of calculations in a fraction of a second, make predictions using computer models of the atmosphere, and update weather maps in a flash whenever new information arrives. Weather satellites can gather data from a vast area of the globe, day after day after day. They can see for thousands of miles and orbit so far above the earth's atmosphere that nothing can interfere with them. By contrast weather ships can only report the conditions at one spot on the ocean's surface, and even meteorological aircraft can cover only a tiny fraction of the earth's surface. Along with the computers and weather satellites, another important factor in forecasting is the global communications network that can carry information from one side of the world to the other in less time than it takes to blink.

The United States launched the first weather satellite in 1960. Called Tiros 1, it took nearly 23,000 photographs of the clouds covering the earth. It was a simple device that always remained lined up on the same point in space, so its cameras only pointed toward the earth for part of each orbit. GOES-1 (or Geostationary Observational Environmental Satellite), launched in 1975, was the first of a family of geostationary weather satellites. These had better equipment and could keep their cameras and other sensors pointing at the earth at all times.

Reliable weather forecasts enable farmers to judge the best time to sow and harvest their crops. The forecasts allow building managers to plan when to switch on heating and air conditioning systems and warn power companies when to expect heavy demand for electricity. Most important of all, the satellites provide flood alerts and hurricane warnings which have saved countless lives and homes.

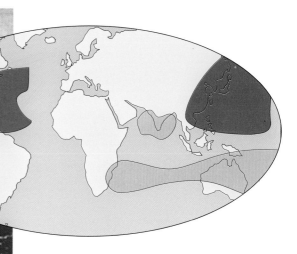

Hurricanes develop over areas of warm ocean water. Areas in red on the map above have an average of more than five hurricanes a year. Areas in pink have up to five hurricanes a year.

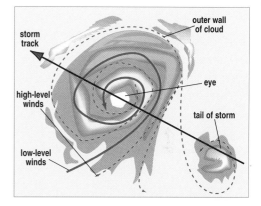

storm track

outer wall of cloud

high-level winds

eye

low-level winds

tail of storm

A fully mature hurricane can be more than 250 miles across, with walls of cloud reaching 10 miles high. The circular bands of cloud produce torrential rainstorms, with winds of 120 miles per hour near the center.

Left: This dramatic picture shows a hurricane system just missing Cuba as it heads westward toward Florida. The picture was taken by the GOES-1 satellite 22,300 miles above South America. Four geostationary satellites, plus three more in polar orbits, provide a 24-hour worldwide weather watch.

Global Air Routes

In the 1920s, when air travel began, aircraft were small and quite slow. In those days, it took a plane almost two days to cross the United States. By the 1950s, the first jets had arrived on the scene, and the same journey could be made in a few hours. Airplanes were no longer just for carrying mail and a few wealthy passengers. Aircraft were getting bigger and faster year by year, and airfares were becoming affordable to millions of people.

By the 1960s, flying had already become the main choice for business travelers. People also began to fly for pleasure, and international tourism took off. Passenger travel doubled and then doubled again. New wide-bodied jets like the Boeing 747 could carry 500 people at a time to destinations all over the world. These days the world's major airlines carry more than 800 million passengers every year.

All this air traffic has to be carefully organized and controlled, and each country has its own official organization to set safety rules and to decide which routes may be used by which airlines. The Federal Aviation Administration (FAA) controls air transport in the United States. The FAA and many other such organizations belong to the International Civil Aviation Organization (ICAO). The ICAO helps airline operators agree on international air routes and standardize their navigation equipment. Air routes–narrow corridors through the air–are plotted on navigation charts. Each route has a set height so, where the routes cross, planes can pass safely above and below one another.

On long flights over the oceans, planes rely mainly on satellite navigation and on their inertial navigation systems. As they approach land, the pilots have more and more radio beacons to guide them, until finally they land under the guidance of the air traffic controllers at the destination airport.

Aircraft come in all shapes and sizes, each specialized for a particular task. The Boeing 747-400 (top left) is a state-of-the-art four-engined jet airliner capable of carrying 500 passengers. The four-engined U.S.-built Lockheed Hercules (above) is one of the world's best-known heavy transport planes. And many international companies use the luxury twin-engined Learjet (below) to ferry their executives around the world.

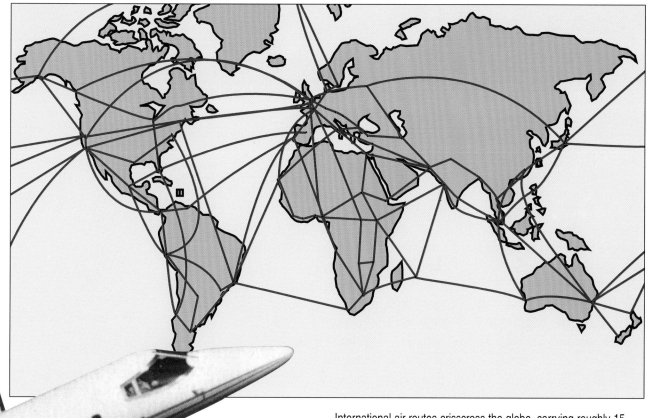

International air routes crisscross the globe, carrying roughly 15 million passengers every week.

International Passengers

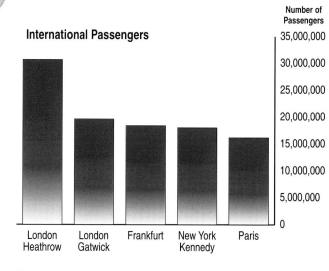

Number of Passengers

- London Heathrow
- London Gatwick
- Frankfurt
- New York Kennedy
- Paris

Based on the number of international passenger arrivals and departures, four of the world's five busiest airports are in Europe. This is because Europe is a hub for both international business travel and tourism.

International and Domestic Passengers

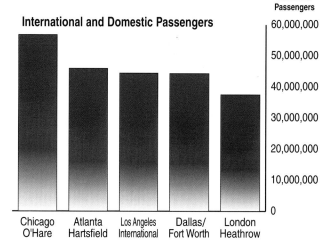

Number of Passengers

- Chicago O'Hare
- Atlanta Hartsfield
- Los Angeles International
- Dallas/ Fort Worth
- London Heathrow

When journeys within the country are counted along with international journeys, four of the five busiest airports are in the United States. This is because the country is very big and has a well-developed domestic airways network.

Have a Good Flight

Airports are like small cities, with their own road systems, waterworks, offices, police forces, fire services, hospitals, shops, and hotels. At a big international airport, there may be 1,200 takeoffs and landings every day, and more than 100,000 people may pass through the terminal buildings. Making it all work efficiently and safely takes thousands of specially trained people.

When the passengers go to the airline desk, their bags are sent down conveyor belts so security staff can check them and put them on the plane. The passengers themselves pass through separate security checks on their way to the departure area. Meanwhile, workers clean the plane, restocking it with meals, beverages, newspapers, and everything else needed for the flight. Engineers also check that all the plane's systems are operating perfectly. Despite all this work, there is often barely an hour between a plane arriving and the same plane leaving again.

Behind the scenes, the pilot, copilot, and flight engineer have collected the air navigation charts they will need for their next flight and are busy preparing their **flight plan** (the summary of the route they will take). The plan gives the reference numbers of the **flight paths** the aircraft will use and lists all the checkpoints along the route, with the distances between them and the estimated time at which the aircraft will pass each one. To complete the plan, the crew obtains up-to-date weather reports for their route from the airport meteorology office. The crew members need to know if they will have a **tailwind** or a **headwind**, because these winds affect the flight time and the amount of fuel required. The pilot also needs to know how many passengers will be on board and how much cargo the plane will be carrying, because the weight of the aircraft also affects the amount of fuel needed.

When the crew has finished all these calculations, the pilot gives a copy of the flight plan to the control tower and transmits a copy to the destination airport so air traffic controllers there know when the flight is due to arrive. Finally the pilot tells the refuelling crew how much fuel to pump into the aircraft's tanks. With the flight planned down to the last detail, the crew is ready to leave.

Main picture: During the final pre-flight check, the flight-deck crew set the navigation instruments and confirm that all the aircraft's systems are fully operational.
Inset: To prepare his detailed flight plan, the pilot studies up-to-the-minute weather reports in the airport meteorological office.

Air Navigation Charts

Aircraft navigation charts are very different from the maps we see in atlases or use for a car journey. Unlike land or sea navigation, air navigation does not rely on landmarks. Land areas are white or pale green, with blue around the coasts fading to white over the oceans. As a result, air navigation charts contain no roads or railroads, towns or rivers. These charts look different for the simple reason that most of the time the aircraft is flying high above the clouds, and the ground is hidden from sight. Even when the skies are clear, the aircraft is usually far too high for details on the ground to be seen clearly. What the chart shows instead is a network of lines (the air routes or corridors) and dozens of circular symbols that indicate the position of radio beacons, which the navigator uses to find the way. For that reason, these maps are called radio navigation charts.

Imagine a Boeing 747 flying from London, England, to Chicago, Illinois. At first the aircraft seems to be heading much too far to the north, but its curving route–called the great circle route–over Scotland, just south of Iceland, over the tip of Greenland, and down to Newfoundland in Canada is actually the shortest distance across the Atlantic.

While an aircraft is over land or within about 200 miles of land, the crew can check the plane's position using the radio beacons and the plane's **distance measuring equipment** (DME). This tool calculates the plane's distance from the beacon by measuring the time it takes for radio signals to go from the beacon to the plane. Other instruments measure the direction of the beacon from the plane, so the instruments can calculate the plane's exact position. In midocean no beacons exist, so the navigator relies on the plane's inertial navigation system.

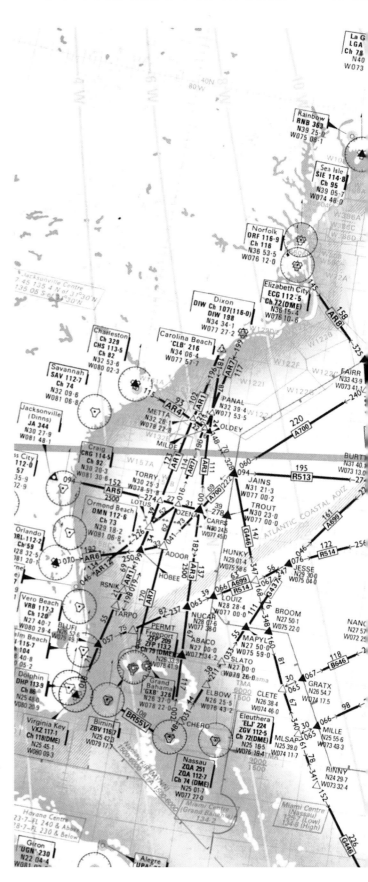

Right: This section of chart North Atlantic (NAT) 2 shows air routes off the eastern coast of the United States. Numbers in rectangular boxes on the lines are route numbers. The numbers above the boxes indicate the number of miles to the next checkpoint. Circles show where the beacons are, and symbols inside the circles describe the type of beacon. Black triangles are control points where the pilot must report in by radio. Open triangles are points where a pilot must report if asked to do so by ground control.

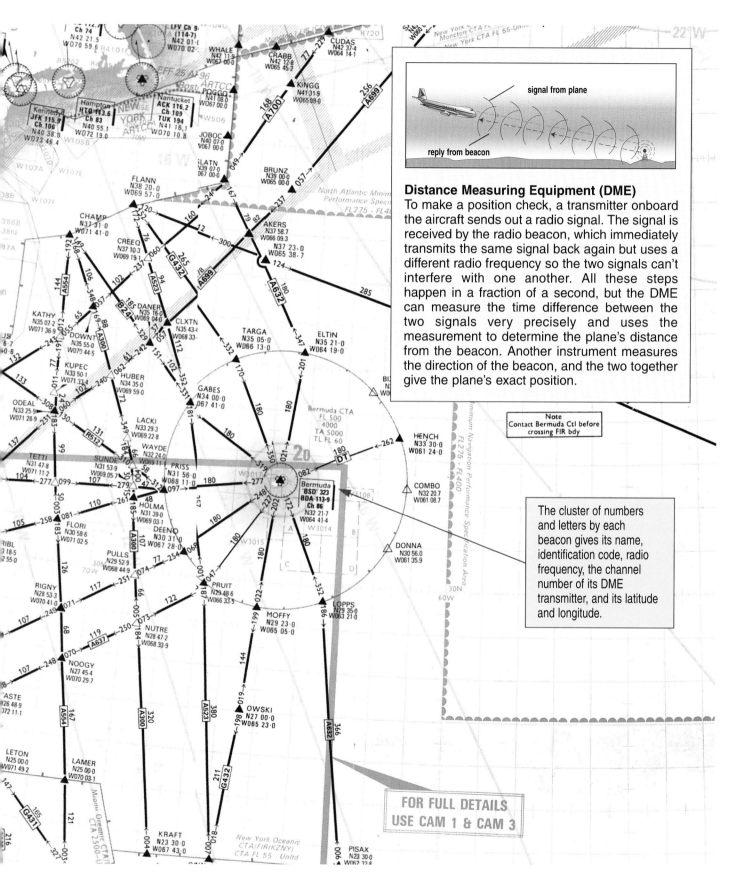

Distance Measuring Equipment (DME)

To make a position check, a transmitter onboard the aircraft sends out a radio signal. The signal is received by the radio beacon, which immediately transmits the same signal back again but uses a different radio frequency so the two signals can't interfere with one another. All these steps happen in a fraction of a second, but the DME can measure the time difference between the two signals very precisely and uses the measurement to determine the plane's distance from the beacon. Another instrument measures the direction of the beacon, and the two together give the plane's exact position.

signal from plane

reply from beacon

Note
Contact Bermuda Ctl before crossing FIR bdy

The cluster of numbers and letters by each beacon gives its name, identification code, radio frequency, the channel number of its DME transmitter, and its latitude and longitude.

FOR FULL DETAILS
USE CAM 1 & CAM 3

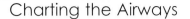
Air Traffic Control

When an aircraft starts to approach land after an ocean crossing, it comes under the authority of air traffic controllers (ATCs) on the ground. The job of ATCs is to make sure that all the planes in their sector get to their destinations quickly and safely. ATCs decide the height at which each plane will fly, the route it will take, and how fast it will fly. If there is a problem–such as fog, ice, or a traffic backup at one airport–ATCs sometimes reroute the planes to alternative airports. At other times, ATCs will order the planes to wait in a stack–a sort of multistory parking lot in the sky some distance away from the airport. Within the stacks, the planes fly around in oval loops, each at a strictly controlled height, until the ATCs tell the planes, in turn, to land. When the plane is ready to leave again, the ATCs will tell the pilot which runway to use, when to take off, how fast to climb, and which air corridor to fly in as the plane leaves the control zone.

The ATCs are based in the control tower at each airport. They usually work in a glass-sided room at the top of the tower, where they have full view of the runways, taxiways, and the aprons alongside the terminal buildings (where the planes park to disembark passengers). The controllers at each airport are responsible for a box of airspace around their airport. No plane may enter or leave that airspace without a proper flight plan and permission from the control tower.

Airspace all over the world is divided into sectors, each under the control of a single ATC center. On a long flight–such as San Diego, California, to New York, New York; Paris, France, to Moscow, Russia; or London, England, to Sydney, Australia–a plane will pass through many different sectors. At the boundary of each one, the aircraft will be handed over from one ATC center to the next.

In many parts of the world, navigators switch to local area charts as they near their destination. Japan, for example, is a mountainous country, so the local area chart for Osaka, one of the country's main airports, shows the hills around the airport as well as the navigation beacons and stacks.

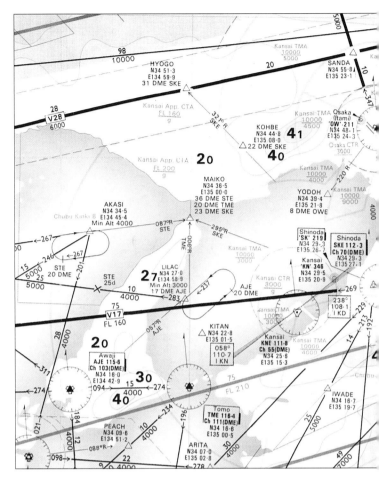

This section of the area chart for Osaka, Japan, shows the high ground around the airport as well as all the radio beacons. The oval shapes over the bay are the stacks used when the airport is busy and planes have to wait their turn to land.

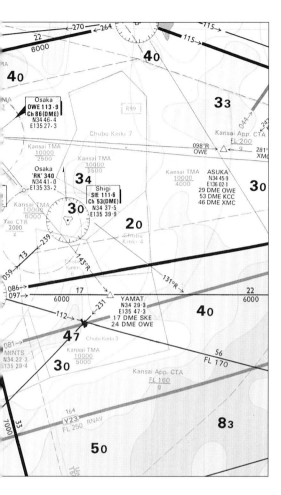

Above: Air traffic control is a very demanding job. ATCs must have total concentration during their time on duty, watching every tiny blip of light on the radar screen to ensure that each plane in the sector is at the correct height, in the correct air corridor, and flying at the correct speed. If an emergency develops–such as a pilot reporting a technical problem or a passenger needing urgent medical attention–the ATCs must react immediately. In a matter of minutes, they will reorganize the air traffic around the airport so that the plane can land.

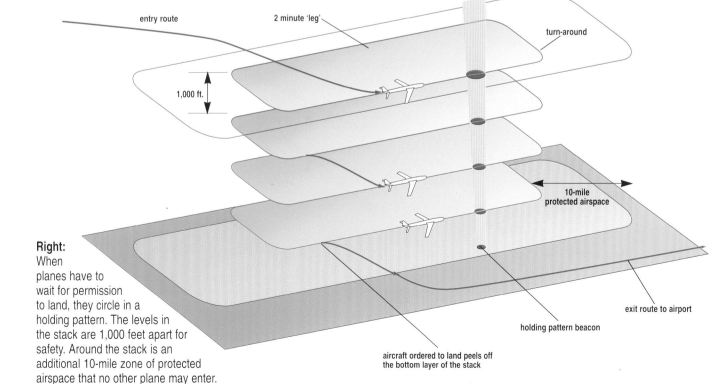

Right: When planes have to wait for permission to land, they circle in a holding pattern. The levels in the stack are 1,000 feet apart for safety. Around the stack is an additional 10-mile zone of protected airspace that no other plane may enter.

Airport Plans

At a big international airport, planes are taking off and landing only a minute or two apart, so the ATCs are constantly busy. In fact the busiest airports usually have two groups of controllers. Approach controllers handle the planes as they come in and land. Ground controllers then take over and tell the pilot which taxiways to use and where to park.

The approach controllers watch each plane carefully, at first on their radar screens and then by eye as soon as the plane is within sight. They tell the pilot from which direction to fly in, how fast to come down, and which runway to use. The pilot can easily follow these instructions using handbooks carried on the plane. For each airport, the books contain charts showing all the different approach routes that can be used, plans of the runways and taxiways, and plans of the airport terminals and parking places.

As the planes come in, the controllers must make sure there is always a safe distance between them. If things get too busy, the approach controllers will place some of the planes in the holding stack until the pressure eases.

If the weather is good and the runway is clearly visible, the pilot will make a visual approach, using instrument readings and visual observations of the runway ahead. But even if the pilot

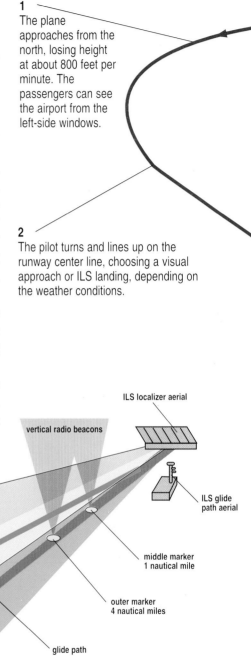

1
The plane approaches from the north, losing height at about 800 feet per minute. The passengers can see the airport from the left-side windows.

2
The pilot turns and lines up on the runway center line, choosing a visual approach or ILS landing, depending on the weather conditions.

ILS localizer aerial

vertical radio beacons

ILS glide path aerial

middle marker
1 nautical mile

outer marker
4 nautical miles

glide path

fly down and right

fly up and left

course correct
on glide path

extended runway center line
(ground level)

Instrument Landing System
The ideal approach line, called the glide path, slopes down at three degrees. About five miles from the airport, the plane picks up the signal from the outer marker beacon. Many airports have a middle and inner beacon, too. These beacons tell pilots how far they are from the runway. The localizer beacon at the far end keeps the plane on the center line, and the glide-path transmitter tells the pilot if the plane is too high or too low.

Landing at Newark Airport

3
The plane touches down on Runway 04R. The reference "04" gives the compass direction of the runway in tens of degrees–in this case 40 degrees measured clockwise from North. The "R" tells the pilot to land on the right-hand runway of the two main runways.

4
With the next plane only a couple of minutes behind, the pilot leaves the runway and taxis toward the airport buildings, following instructions from the control tower.

5
The plane parks at the International Arrivals terminal, and the passengers disembark.

Below: General airport plans show the size and shape of the airport and the size of the main runways.

can't see the ground at all because of fog or snow, the plane can still land safely with its **instrument landing system** (ILS). The ILS system uses the signals from radio beacons on the runway to guide the plane down through the air and onto the runway. If the plane is too high or too low or a bit to the left or right of the runway center line, visual displays and bleeper signals tell the pilot what adjustments to make.

As soon as the aircraft has landed, the ground controllers inform the pilot of the assigned taxiway so that the runway can be cleared quickly to make room for the next plane. All taxiways are numbered, and at night small colored lights embedded in the concrete illuminate the paths.

Glossary

air navigation chart: A special chart used for navigating aircraft. The chart shows air lanes, airports, and radio beacons but no detail of what is on the ground.

bearing: The compass direction of one place from another. Bearings are normally given as the number of degrees measured clockwise (East) from North. A bearing can also be given in degrees West of North, but in that case it must say so clearly. For example, southwest would usually be written as "bearing 225 degrees" or "225°," but it could also be written "bearing 135 degrees West" (135°W).

crosswind: A wind blowing from the side of a ship or aircraft. A crosswind pushes the craft off course, so the navigator heads slightly into the wind to compensate.

current: A stream of water or air.

distance measuring equipment (DME): Radio equipment on board an aircraft that calculates the plane's exact position using signals from radio beacons on the ground.

flight path: The path taken through the air by an airplane or spacecraft.

flight plan: A list of route numbers and checkpoints showing the route an aircraft will take from one airport to another.

headwind: A wind blowing from in front of a ship or aircraft, slowing it down.

inertial navigation: A fully automatic navigation system that keeps track of the position of a ship or aircraft by measuring every change in speed and direction from the vessel's starting point.

instrument landing system (ILS): A group of instruments on board a plane that listens to signals from radio transmitters at the airport and that helps the pilot make a safe landing, even if the airport is hidden by fog.

knot: The unit used for measuring the speed of a ship or airplane. One knot is a speed of one nautical mile an hour.

latitude: Distance north or south of the equator, measured as an angle from the center of the earth.

lead line: A rope or wire with a heavy lead weight on the end that is used for measuring water depth.

longitude: Distance east or west of a line running through Greenwich, London, England. Lines of longitude encircle the earth from north to south, passing through the North and South Poles.

marine chronometer: A clock or watch designed to work accurately at sea, even when a ship is pitching and tossing.

nautical mile: The unit of distance used by sea and air navigators. The internationally agreed value, which has been used by the U.S. since 1959, is 6,076.115 feet (1,852 meters).

pilot log: A device that calculates the speed of a ship by measuring the pressure of the water as the ship pushes through it.

position line: Any line on a map or chart used to pinpoint the position of a ship or aircraft.

radio direction finding (RDF): Any method of fixing the position of a ship or aircraft using radio signals from transmitters (beacons) on land.

reflecting quadrant: A navigation instrument used to measure the angle between the horizon and the sun, the moon, or a star. The reflecting quadrant was a forerunner of the sextant.

sea chart: A chart used for navigating a ship, small boat, or submarine. The chart shows the water depth, submerged rocks, and the position of buoys, lighthouses, radio beacons, and other navigation aids.

sextant: A navigation instrument used for measuring the angle between the horizon and a celestial body such as the sun, the moon, or a star.

sonar: Equipment for calculating distance underwater by transmitting sound waves and then measuring the time it takes for the waves to bounce back from the seabed or other solid objects underwater. The name comes from *SO*und *N*avigation *A*nd *R*anging.

sun sight (star sight): The measurement of the angle between the horizon and the sun or a star.

tailwind: A wind blowing from behind a ship or aircraft, making it go faster.

Index

A

air navigation charts, 38, 40, 41, 42
air traffic controller, 42, 43
almanac, 17
altitude, 17
astrolabe, 11, 16
azimuth circle, 14

B

beacon, 18, 40, 41, 42, 43, 44, 45
bearing, 7, 13, 14, 15
buoy, 14, 18, 29

C

celestial bodies, 16, 17
celestial navigation, 16, 17
chip log, 12, 13
chronometer, 11
Columbus, Christopher, 11, 22
compass, 7, 8, 10, 11, 12, 14, 20, 21, 45
Cook, Captain James, 22
cross-staff, 16, 17
crosswinds, 12
currents, 12, 22, 23, 24, 28, 29, 32, 33

D

dead reckoning, 12, 13
Dias, Bartolomeu, 11
distance measuring equipment (DME), 40, 41

E

El Niño, 32
equator, 8, 10, 28, 29, 32

F

Federal Aviation Administration (FAA), 36
flight path, 38
flight plan, 38, 42

G

Gama, Vasco da, 11
geologist, 30, 31

geology, 7, 23, 30
GOES-1, 34, 35
gyres, 28
gyrocompass, 20, 21
gyroscope, 20

H

headland, 8, 14, 28
headwind, 38
horizon, 8, 9, 16, 17

I

inertial navigation, 20, 36, 40,
instrument landing system (ILS), 44, 45
International Civil Aviation Organization (ICAO), 36

K

knot-meter, 13

L

latitude, 10, 11, 16, 29, 41
lead line, 22, 24
lighthouse, 14, 15, 18
longitude, 11, 41
Loran, 18

M

Magellan, Ferdinand, 22
magnetic compass, 11
marine chronometer, 11
Maury, Matthew Fontaine, 24
meteorological aircraft, 34

N

navigating, 7, 11, 12, 13, 14, 18, 20, 24, 25, 26,
navigation channel, 14
Navstar, 18
North Star, 16

O

oceanography, 22, 23
Omega, 18

P

pelorus, 14
periscope, 20
piloting, 14
plankton, 30, 32

position line, 14
protractor, 14

Q

quadrant, 16, 17

R

radar, 7, 14, 18, 19, 44
radio direction finding, 18
reef, 14, 15

S

sandbank, 14, 27, 31
sandglass, 12, 13
satellite, 7, 9, 13, 18, 20, 23, 32, 34, 35, 36
sea chart, 11, 12, 14, 47
seafarer, 8, 10
seafloor, 7, 22, 23, 25, 27, 30
sextant, 7, 16, 17
sighting bar, 16
sonar, 13, 24, 25, 26, 27, 29
star sight, 17, 20

T

tailwind, 38
telescope, 14
Tiros 1, 34

W

wreck 14, 15, 27

48